BLUE'S RIVER

Kathleen M Doyle

Delaware
& Surrounding Lands & Water

Pennsylvania

Delaware River

New Castle County

New Jersey

Maryland

Kent County

Delaware Bay

Sussex County

Atlantic Ocean

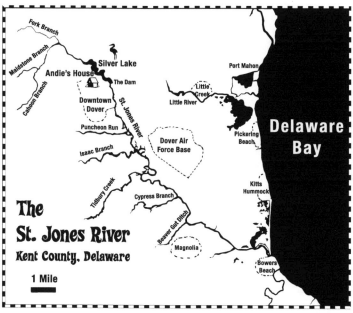

The St. Jones River
Kent County, Delaware

Fork Branch

Maidstone Branch

Silver Lake

Andie's House

Port Mahon

The Dam

Cahoon Branch

Downtown Dover

Little Creek

Little River

St. Jones River

Puncheon Run

Dover Air Force Base

Pickering Beach

Delaware Bay

Isaac Branch

Tidbury Creek

Kitts Hummock

Cypress Branch

Beaver Gut Ditch

Magnolia

Bowers Beach

1 Mile

BLUE'S RIVER

Written by Kathleen Marie Doyle

Illustrated by Marsha Holler

ISBN: 978-1-7340432-0-4

Illustrations copyright © 2019 Marsha Holler

Ordinary Artichoke Medium font courtesy of Joette

www.happyselfpublisher.com

Note:

Some places, names, and dates from Dover, Delaware's recent history have been slightly altered. Historical events, names, and places prior to the 21st century are meant to be accurate, and if they are not, the fault lies entirely with the author.

Blue's River is dedicated to Mrs. Carlson, my 5th grade teacher,
and to all the teachers who patiently put up with me.

Table of Contents

CHAPTER 1

Panic

Andie Grove was afraid of only one thing.

"We will start with volunteers."

The dread that had been sitting on Andie's chest all day now spread up her throat and down her legs. Her knees felt weak. She knew Mrs. Carlson would accept no excuses this time. The school year would be over in three weeks, and then Andie would be an official 6th grader — but first, she had to pass this presentation.

Mrs. Carlson was always telling students to overcome their fears. Try new things. Take risks. Dream big. This stupid presentation had to be about a big dream they had for the future. Easy for Mrs. Carlson to say. She probably always wanted to be a teacher — and of course teachers love doing presentations.

Mrs. Carlson had been Andie's all-time favorite

teacher — until now. Andie was sure she could get through life without ever having to do a speech. After all, she had managed to avoid it this far.

Three students raised their hands, including Andie's best friend, Lily Sanchez, who sat next to Andie. Mrs. Carlson chose Lily.

Lily was smart, confident, and pretty. Today, her straight dark hair was pulled into two perfect braids. Andie's own mop of short brown curls was wild and could not be tamed. The only thing she liked about her hair was that it added an inch of height to her small four-foot frame.

Kids used to tease her for being short, but that stopped last year when Andie's triumphant kick scored three runs, winning the end-of-year fourth-grade versus fifth-grade kickball game. This year, in physical education class, everyone wanted her on their team. If only public speaking were as easy as kickball.

The students were required to have props with their presentation, and Lily had two: the purple scrubs she wore and the toy stethoscope around her neck. Andie had no props because she had no presentation. She was in her usual oversized tee-shirt, baggy shorts and red high tops.

Andie's hands were clenched in fear that Mrs. Carlson might choose her. She could barely think it made her so nervous. To distract herself, she thought about all the things she loved to do. She loved to read, write, solve math problems, climb trees, hang out with her baby sister Emma, and learn about what was going on in the world. She just couldn't talk in front of a group of people.

"My dream," Lily began, "is to become a veterinarian. I have loved animals since the day I was born. How many of you have pets?"

Lily made it look so easy. The fear in Andie's chest made it hard to breathe.

Lily finished her presentation in exactly two minutes — the required time limit. Mrs. Carlson praised Lily for her loud voice, her eye contact, and for memorizing her presentation.

Andie held her breath, praying that someone else would volunteer. Jeffrey Johnson raised his hand. For the first time ever, Andie felt grateful for Jeffrey Johnson. Jeffrey walked confidently to the front of the room carrying a bike helmet.

"I am already living my dream because I have a better bike than everybody in this room, and I can do more tricks than all of you put together."

Lily snuck a sideways glance at Andie. Andie rolled her eyes and Lily smiled. Jeffrey was always bragging. He went on to list all the tricks he could do and the races he had won. Mrs. Carlson let him continue even though he passed the two-minute mark. When he finished, she praised him for his enthusiasm.

"Okay, who's next?" Mrs. Carlson asked. "We need to have four presentations each day until next Tuesday."

Silence.

"Andie Grove, would you like to get it over with? You will feel so much better once you are done."

Andie stopped breathing. Tears spilled down her cheeks. Jeffrey Johnson snickered and whispered something to his neighbor.

Mrs. Carlson walked to Andie's desk and crouched down to be at eye level with her small student.

She said quietly, "I'm sorry, Andie. I will let you volunteer when you are ready." Andie choked through her tears and asked if she could go to the nurse.

Mrs. Carlson chose Jamal Scott to present next.

Andie could feel everyone staring at her as she walked out of the room. She closed the door behind her and began to sob.

CHAPTER 2

Old Blue

Old Blue had lived on the Saint Jones River in Dover, Delaware, for centuries. He had helped raise hundreds, maybe thousands, of great blue herons, and now he had two more who had just taken their first flights and were learning to find their own food. Old Blue should have felt relaxed now that he no longer had to spend hours each day hunting and fishing for the endless amount of food his offspring required.

Unfortunately, Old Blue had not felt relaxed in many years. Long ago, the river was healthy, teeming with many varieties of fish. Finding food was never a problem. He fished in the salt water along the coast and tidal flats, as well as in fresh water rivers, ponds, and marshes. For variety, the occasional snake or mouse sometimes made a good feast. These days, however, he felt embarrassed about having to resort to stealing fish from people's backyard ponds.

Old Blue had studied humans all his life. They were fascinating, complicated, brilliant creatures who loved to invent new machines and new ideas. They could also be clueless, careless, and cruel.

The first humans who settled along the river delighted in all the waterway had to offer. They knew that their lives depended on the river. Later settlers took a different view and believed the river was theirs to own and control. They cut down trees, straightened the river's course, filled in the wetlands, and put houses where the marshes used to be. They built dams and mills that used the river's current for energy. They developed chemicals which ended up in the river and in the bodies of the animals that relied on the river for their food. Humans even used the river as a dump for their garbage and sewage.

Old Blue shook his dark plumed head. He felt a great responsibility to protect his river. The animals, birds, and the fish looked to him for guidance. Once upon a time, even humans looked to the Great Blue Heron for wisdom.

For hundreds of years, people had taken the river for granted, but some positive changes were now happening. Humans had learned from some of their mistakes. They no longer built houses on wetlands. They now understood the importance of planting trees to stop erosion along the river banks. They were bringing back native plants which helped to absorb and filter rainwater as it made its way into the ground. Many farmers were more careful about when and how they fertilized their crops. Legislators were passing new laws to protect the environment.

Old Blue felt a glimmer of hope, but he was tired. He was ready to pass the feather on to a new river guardian.

Diving Deeper

Great blue herons are not picky eaters. They mostly eat fish but if they are hungry enough, they will eat almost any small animal — even a baby alligator!

They live near lakes, rivers, swamps and marshes.

They fish in fresh water and in salt water.

CHAPTER 3

First Encounter

When the bell rang at 2:30 to dismiss all walkers, Andie shuffled slowly from the nurse's office toward her locker, hoping to avoid her classmates. Usually she and Lily walked home together, but this week, Lily's grandmother was picking her up every day. Lily's mother was in Texas making a big presentation at a medical conference. Lily's parents were divorced, and her father lived in Massachusetts. Whenever Lily's mom needed to travel for work, Lily stayed with her grandmother.

"Nice job today, Grover!"

The sarcastic voice behind her belonged to Jeffrey Johnson. Andie felt like slugging him, a skill she had learned from her brother Harry who was two years older. Instead, she slammed her locker shut and ignored him. Fortunately, Jeffrey was in a hurry to get on his bicycle and did not linger.

The May sun was warm, but Andie barely noticed.

Her hometown of Dover, the capital of Delaware, was always beautiful in the spring, even though the season's vibrant pinks, purples and yellows had begun to fade. All she could think about was how she never wanted to go back to school.

She decided that a stop at Silver Lake to skip stones might make her feel better. She and Lily often raced each other to the lake to play on the swings. Andie always won. Recently, Lily had suggested they were getting too old for swings, but as long as Andie could still jump off the swing at its highest point and land softly (a benefit of being small), she was going to keep swinging. One week from today would be Memorial Day, and the lake would finally be open for swimming after the long winter. Even Lily couldn't think they were too old for that.

A light breeze rustled the leaves of the trees that stood guard around Silver Lake. In the distance, water splashed over the concrete dam into the Saint Jones River. Nearby, several small children were shouting happily from the bright yellow and blue plastic playground. Andie's feet made a soft crunching sound as she walked onto the small sandy beach. Grass was growing through the beach sand which made the beach look as though it had been deserted longer than just eight months.

Andie did not know she was being watched as she poked around in the sand looking for a few good skipping stones. The right stone had to be flat and fit perfectly between her thumb and forefinger. She found three good ones, but they all sank without a single skip.

"It figures," she muttered.

She spied a crumpled plastic water bottle floating near the shoreline. "What is wrong with people?" she said out loud as she pulled the bottle ashore using a long stick. She normally would have waded in to get it, but she was wearing her brand new red high tops and didn't feel like fussing with the laces. She began to examine the sand more closely and noticed candy wrappers, cigarette butts, and a soda can. Just a few yards away, a grocery bag was caught in a bush.

To get to the bag, Andie needed to climb up some rocks and squeeze through two holly bushes. She walked backwards through the bushes to avoid getting hit in the face by the sharp pointy leaves. Before she could turn back around, a quiet voice whispered, "Hello there!"

Andie froze.

The voice said, "You need not be frightened."

Andie turned around slowly. Standing before her, a little taller than Andie, was a prehistoric looking bird with piercing golden eyes and a large yellow spear-like beak. His crown was white, and his shoulders looked like black shoulder pads holding long grey and blue plumes in place. A black mask of feathers surrounded his piercing eyes which were staring down into Andie's face. His legs were long and stick thin, ending in comically large feet. Three of his toes faced forward while the fourth stuck out in back. He had a bald spot on his breast just below his right wing.

"Do not be alarmed. I am Old Blue. Thank you for caring about my river."

Andie was indeed alarmed, but recovered quickly.

"You're welcome," she said, "But this is a lake, not a river."

"This lake was the river before it was the lake,"

Old Blue replied.

Andie found this to be quite confusing, but not as confusing as a talking bird.

"My river and your lake are in peril and that means that you and I are in trouble. This has been my home for 400 years. I have raised many chicks on this river, but a great many of my relatives have moved away."

"Did you say '400 years'?" Andie asked.

"I did indeed. Hence, the name Old Blue," he replied proudly. "Most of my species only live to about 20 years old. They are considered quite elderly if they make it to 23!"

Andie's mind was racing. A 400-year-old talking bird? If only Lily were here! Although Lily had become so sensible, that she would probably tell this bird to have a good day and yank Andie away.

"Would you care to take a tour of what my river looked like 400 years ago?" Old Blue asked.

A 400-year-old talking bird who could travel back in time? The only thing Andie could think of saying was, "Will I be back in time for dinner?"

Old Blue replied, "No one will realize you were gone."

Andie didn't know whether to feel happy or sad about his last comment, but for some reason, she trusted this strange bird. Besides, after the day she had, she needed an adventure.

Diving Deeper

Great blue herons:

Their height ranges from 3.5 feet to 4.5 feet.
Their average weight is 5 pounds.
Their average lifespan is 15 years.
They can fly between 20 and 30 miles per hour.

Ten-year old girls:

Their height ranges from 4 feet to 5 feet.
Their average weight is 70.5 pounds.
Their average life span (worldwide) is 72 years.
They cannot fly on their own.

CHAPTER 4

The Lenape

Andie swung her leg over Old Blue's back, wrapped her arms around his S shaped neck as gently as she could and tucked her feet behind his wings. Old Blue took two slow steps forward, dipping low to the ground with each step. Andie began to slide back. "Hold tighter! You will not break me!" He spread his wings to their full five-foot span, flapped three times, and the two travelers were airborne. Andie's worries gave way to excitement.

Andie had never been in an airplane, never mind on the back of a bird. She squeezed her eyes shut and pressed her face into the soft blue, gray, and white feathers of his neck. As his wings settled into a rhythm, Andie grew more relaxed. She peeked out of her left eye and saw the group of houses that formed her neighborhood. She lifted her head slightly, opened both eyes and saw the highway off to the east. Below, the lake narrowed into a river.

Soon they were flying over the remains of the old high school which had long stood vacant, waiting to be torn down. They passed over the old power plant which used to burn coal and then oil, sending black smoke through its stacks.

Old Blue soared above the treetops, and followed the outline of the river. The river branched off into smaller tributaries in several places. As the great blue heron ascended higher, everything on the ground grew smaller. Tiny cars inched along narrow roads which crisscrossed each other. Housing developments and strip malls looked like board game pieces. The landscape grew distant until Andie was enveloped in a mist.

Soon they were flying above a white carpet of clouds surrounded by blue sky. The air was cool and clean. Andie felt giddy with excitement. When they emerged below the clouds, she could not believe her eyes. A lush forest of elm, oak and hickory trees now stood where roads, houses, and strip malls had been moments earlier.

As Old Blue flew lower, Andie could see the river

through the trees. Then she saw the huts and the people.

Old Blue spied a good landing branch high in the forest canopy. "Hold tight!"

He was surprisingly graceful for such a large, gangly bird. He glided through an opening in the trees just large enough for his five-foot wingspan and his passenger. He then straightened his legs and wrapped his long toes around a large branch. Smaller branches brushed Andie's legs, and several leaves landed in her curls. One of Old Blue's feathers came loose and drifted to a branch below.

"Welcome to Mitsawokett!" Old Blue said. "I believe my memory is accurate. That was the name the Lenape gave to the river and this area."

Andie had learned about the Lenape tribe in Mrs. Carlson's class. It was one of her favorite topics. She could not believe she was seeing Lenape people as they actually lived 400 years ago.

From their perch, Andie and Old Blue were close enough to see the clear river was filled with fish. A few feet from the shore, three small dark-haired children

splashed and shrieked with delight.

Three women chatted nearby while they kept close watch over the children. One of the women was filling clay pots with water. Another was seated, weaving a basket out of willow twigs. The third woman was pounding grain with a stone.

Under a nearby tree, a man with a long braid was using a sharp tool to hollow out a long log. A stone-tipped spear and a bow and arrow were propped up against the tree. Nearby, two canoes and a net made from woven grasses lay on the ground.

A short distance away, some trees had been cleared. Andie saw a cluster of huts. Some were small and others were long.

"Those small huts are called 'wigwams,'" Old Blue said. "They are for a single family. The larger ones are called 'long houses.' They can fit several families."

A pile of furs was stacked outside one of the wigwams. Behind the homes, crops were beginning to sprout in a small plot of land about the size of Andie's backyard.

Suddenly, the tree began to vibrate, and Andie heard a rumbling sound. The man below grabbed the bow and arrow and dashed into the woods.

"Are we having an earthquake?" she asked nervously. She had felt a light earthquake once, but this one felt different.

"No, it is a stampede of bison."

"Bison?" Andie asked with doubt in her voice. She looked carefully at Old Blue. "There are no bison in Delaware!"

Old Blue shook his head sadly. "You are correct. Bison have been gone for a very long time. As more humans settled here and cleared the land, the bison and other animals lost their habitat and were forced to move."

Andie hesitated before asking her next question. "What happened to the Lenape people?"

"Many moved away, some died from disease and others were forced out. Europeans and their descendants began moving here, claiming the land as their own. The Lenape were pressured to leave, and eventually their

24

chief sold the land to an Englishman. Only a few stayed. Their descendants live in Dover and other towns along the Saint Jones today."

Andie was quiet as she absorbed this information. After a few minutes of silence, the forest grew dark. A cloud had blocked the sun. A gust of wind dislodged the feather from the branch below. As the feather floated down toward the river, one of the children saw it and raced out of the water to try to catch it. The child gazed up into the trees.

Andie whispered, "Can she see us?"

Old Blue replied, "Children usually can."

The child smiled and splashed back into the river waving the long blue feather.

Joy swept over Andie. What a day! Had she really spent part of it in tears? She looked at her watch. It had stopped at 3:20.

"Do not fret about the time. I will show you one more place today, and I shall return you home in time for your evening meal. Hold on!"

Old Blue crouched down and sprang through the

25

small canopy opening. The three children below stopped playing and watched as Andie and her new friend rose gracefully above the forest and into the clouds.

Diving Deeper

Before Europeans settled in Delaware, the Lenni-Lenape — or Lenape (pronounced *le-NAH-pay*) lived in Delaware, north of Cape Henlopen (along the entire Delaware Bay), and in eastern Pennsylvania, as well as New Jersey, and southeastern New York.

Some historians refer to the Lenape as the "trunk" from which many other Native American tribes branched. Native communities prefer to emphasize the importance of family relationships among tribes. They refer to the Lenape as the grandfather nation (rather than the trunk) of the many distinct Native American Algonquian speaking tribes.

Many people from the Lenape and Nanticoke communities in Delaware moved to New Jersey during the late 19th and early 20th centuries to escape restrictive racial laws. A newer sister tribe is the Nanticoke Lenni Lenape Nation, a group of Native communities in Cumberland and Salem Counties in New Jersey.

CHAPTER 5

Slavery, Soil, and the Saint Jones

The Lenape huts were gone. Alternating acres of bright green fields and barren brown patches now appeared along the river that had once cut through a great forest. Deep ditches lined the fields. Small log houses dotted the landscape. Trees burned in the distance.

"They are burning the trees to clear the land for farming," Old Blue explained.

As the pair flew closer, Andie saw people working in the fields, harvesting big green leaves. "Are those people slaves?" she asked, fearing she already knew the answer.

"Most are probably enslaved, although some might be indentured servants. By this time, the three counties that eventually became known as Delaware had hundreds, perhaps thousands of enslaved humans."

"By what time?"

"I have brought you to the year 1722. Slavery has been in this area for approximately 80 years by this point, and will last an additional 143 years."

Andie shook her head sadly. How could people ever think it was okay to make other people their slaves?

"What is that crop they are picking? It looks like little lettuce trees."

"That is tobacco," Old Blue replied. "It was a very valuable and labor intensive crop. For a short while, farmers grew very rich since they did not pay their workers. Unfortunately, the farmers were not particularly knowledgeable about soil."

Andie asked Old Blue to explain.

"Tobacco needs certain nutrients that only exist in fresh soil. Once it gets all the nutrients out of the soil, the soil becomes infertile and needs a long rest — sometimes many years before anything new can grow. That's why you see so many empty fields. That also explains why they are burning trees to clear more land."

"What are the ditches for?" Andie asked.

29

Old Blue answered, "The ditches drained the water from the marshland, drying the area out so that crops could be planted."

They continued to fly along the river. Andie had been so focused on the people in the fields that she had not noticed the cows, pigs, goats, and sheep wandering in and along the river.

"What are those animals doing?" she exclaimed. "Why aren't they in barns?"

"Ah yes, those fellows are yet another reason for empty fields. The farmers were unable to manage all the animals they brought over from Europe. Over time, there were so many animals, the farmers were forced to let them roam free. The animals trampled the fields and wandered into the marshes, river, and forest. All that stomping ravaged the soil. Large storms washed the topsoil into the river. You cannot grow crops without healthy topsoil."

Andie was troubled that the farmers would enslave people yet set animals free. She decided, however, not to share this thought with Old Blue.

Old Blue continued to fly over farmland. In the distance Andie noticed several buildings clustered close together. They looked like a small town. As they got closer, Andie thought the area looked familiar.

"Is that The Green?" she asked. Her family often walked there to hear concerts, and they never missed the annual Dover Days celebration on The Green.

"Not yet, but you have the right location. You are witnessing the early stages of what was called the 'Public Square' which will someday be renamed 'The Green.'"

A brick building with a porch stood where Andie was used to seeing the Old State House. On the southwest corner was a log house, stable, and pasture. Three horses were grazing in the pasture, and laughter rang from inside the log house.

"Believe it or not, that old log tavern was the first real courthouse in Kent County. They built it in 1699, but humans wanted something a little more dignified, so they built this brick courthouse which was just finished this year."

"Is that State Street?" Andie asked, pointing to a

31

dirt road next to the old log tavern.

Old Blue answered, "Eventually it will be known as 'State Street.' Right now, it is called 'The King's Highway', and it is the main road. Remember, the King of England is still the ruler."

Andie thought it did not look like much of a highway. She tried to imagine a king so close to her house, riding in his carriage pulled by majestic horses. Horse-drawn buggies were not unusual in Dover because of the Amish, but a king was something else entirely. She wondered why, nowadays, there was still a street in Dover called King's Highway.

Old Blue continued, "The real highways at this time were the rivers, but The King's Highway was the main road from Philadelphia to Lewes."

Andie studied the scene below and realized that the river was wider and swampier than in modern times.

Old Blue said, "The dam at Silver Lake has not yet been built. Once it is established, the river will narrow below the dam and pool above the dam to form a lake. In later years, humans will fill in the wetlands so that they can construct buildings. They did that in numerous places throughout the area."

"Won't the buildings sink?"

"No," Old Blue replied. "But they might flood. Don't worry, humans have learned from that mistake, and they are more careful with the wetlands in your time."

"Is the river called 'the Saint Jones' yet?"

"Yes, it is. For a time, it was known as 'Wolf's Creek,' because so many wolves drank and hunted on its shores, but it came to be called 'Saint Jones' in the 1670s. There was a fellow named Robert Jones who owned a large amount of land by the river, and I am quite certain that is how it got its name, but humans are still debating where the name came from."

"I've never heard about wolves around here," Andie stated.

Old Blue replied, "Like many animals that used to live here, the wolves were hunted, trapped, and pushed out as their habitat disappeared."

Andie asked Old Blue, "Why don't you hate people? We have done such horrible things — to people, animals, and nature!"

Old Blue replied, "The wonderful thing about humans is that you seem to learn from your mistakes."

Andie was not so sure about this.

Old Blue spied a wooded area behind the new courthouse.

"Let's find some shade, shall we?"

He landed on a patch of grass, and Andie slid off his back. The two friends walked toward the woods. Old Blue's strides were long but slow. Andie had no trouble keeping up with him.

"So," Andie began, "the Lenape were forced to leave, African people were enslaved, trees were burned and replaced by fields, and the bison and wolves disappeared. Out of everything I've seen so far, the only thing that seems good, I guess, is that the Public Square was built. Is that it?"

Old Blue threw back his head and let out a loud

shriek. The sound was quite frightening. Andie wondered if he was laughing at her.

"Where to begin?" Old Blue said.

Diving Deeper

No one knows with certainty how the Saint Jones River got its name. Some people believe the river was named after Saint John but with a Welsh spelling (Saint Jone). Others believe the name came from transcripts which read "said Jones" abbreviated to "sd Jones" eventually becoming St. Jones.

Herons have much better eyesight than humans and can see clearly both in daylight and at night. The location of their eyes on the sides of their head allows them to see what is in front of them and what is behind them.

CHAPTER 6

The Three Lower Counties

As Andie and Old Blue strolled slowly toward the woods, Old Blue told Andie about more events that happened between the time of the Lenape and the creation of the Public Square in Dover.

"For a time, humans from the Netherlands, then Sweden, and then the Netherlands again, claimed this region as their own. After the Dutch recaptured the region, it became part of New York, and then in 1682, the area became part of Pennsylvania. When the Swedes were here, they were the people who called our river 'Wolf's Creek'."

Just when Andie realized that the shadow on the ground in front of her could not belong to an airplane, an enormous bald eagle zoomed toward them. The heron squawked and stumbled toward the woods, his wings thrashing the air. Andie tried to keep up with Old Blue, but she fell behind. Fortunately, the eagle was not interested in Andie. It lost sight of Old Blue, and swooped away in disappointment.

Old Blue was breathing heavily when Andie caught up to him. She said, "I can't believe any bird is crazy enough to try to mess with someone as big as you!"

Old Blue replied, "I have only a few enemies, and the bald eagle is one of them. I am taller than most eagles, but their wings are much wider, they weigh twice as much as I do, and they can fly twice as fast. I fought one off when I was young, but I am less foolish now and would rather run than fight."

Andie asked Old Blue if the scar on his breast had come from an eagle. "No, this is from a great horned owl. Those owls are as dreadful as the eagles."

Andie looked around and wondered what other creatures might be lurking in the shadows. Wolves? Bison?

"Now then, where was I?" Old Blue continued. "In 1682, William Penn changed the name of this county from 'Saint Jones County' to 'Kent County.' Pennsylvania was a British colony, and Delaware was part of it."

Andie interrupted. "Wait! So, first we were New York, then we were Pennsylvania, then we were Delaware?"

Old Blue answered, "More or less, except before Delaware became 'Delaware,' it was known as 'The Lower Three Counties of Pennsylvania on the Delaware'."

Andie wondered how people would have fit all that on an envelope. She was glad the name was eventually shortened.

"Delaware was not yet its own colony, but by

1722, William Penn had grown weary of the lower three counties' constant complaints about how they were ignored by the leaders further north. In fact, he actually had been ignoring them, leaving them to fend for themselves against pirates and attacks from Maryland."

"Pirates!" Andie exclaimed. "I always thought pirates were make-believe."

"Not at all," Old Blue said. "Pirates were quite common. They would hide along the shore, waiting to plunder merchant ships carrying valuable items. Sometimes they even came ashore to steal, or kidnap, or both."

Old Blue continued, "Eventually, Penn reluctantly allowed the lower three counties to rule themselves with their own General Assembly. The governor of Pennsylvania was still officially in charge of the lower three counties, but he mostly left them alone. Once the three lower counties were permitted to rule themselves, it was only a matter of time before they would break away completely."

"How do you remember all this history?" Andie asked.

"I lived it! Besides, studying humans is a fascinating way to pass the time."

The silence of the Public Square was broken by two men talking loudly as they walked from the tavern toward the courthouse. They wore long waistcoats, short pants, and white stockings up to their knees. Andie giggled when she realized they were wearing white wigs — just like in the posters in Mrs. Carlson's classroom.

On the other side of the courthouse, two women strolled arm in arm. They looked younger than Andie's mother and wore their hair piled high on their heads. Their dresses were long and layered. The skirts fit tightly at the waist, but fell wide and stiff near the hem. Andie wondered how they could walk so close together with such wide skirts. She was grateful that she lived in a time when she could wear tee-shirts, shorts, and sneakers.

Old Blue interrupted her thoughts. "I do believe it is time we returned home, so climb aboard."

Exhaustion and elation filled Andie as the two travelers entered the clouds. She had experienced over one hundred years of history in one afternoon. She wondered how long they had actually been gone.

Old Blue dropped Andie off where he had picked her up. The same children were still playing at the playground. Andie looked at her watch. It had resumed ticking. The time was 3:20.

Diving Deeper

In 1683, William Penn gave the name "Dover" to a town which had not yet been built. He probably named it after Dover in Kent County, England. In a written order, he described how he wanted the town laid out, including how wide the streets should be and where the courthouse and jail should be located. In 1717, the Public Square (later called The Green) was finally laid out, mostly in accordance with Penn's 1683 instructions.

New Castle County and Sussex County were mostly settled by immigrants new to the colonies, while Kent County was settled mostly by people from Maryland.

CHAPTER 7

The Groves

Andie took the shortcut home through the old African-American cemetery. A pot of vibrant red geraniums stood by one tombstone, and a bouquet of purple plastic tulips leaned against another. Deflated balloons draped a third stone. Faded silk flowers and flags adorned several other stones in the small graveyard. Many stones were so old and weather-beaten that the names and dates were impossible to read. A few had fallen over. Andie wondered if any people buried here had been alive in the 1600s or 1700s. Would any of them have been enslaved?

When Andie arrived home, she heard her mother talking on the phone in the kitchen. She took a quick look in the hallway mirror and noticed several leaves and a twig stuck in her hair. She quickly brushed them out with her fingers.

Three-year-old Emma was sitting at the kitchen

table munching on some apple slices and peanut butter when she spied her sister. "Andie!" she shouted gleefully as she slid off the chair to give her sister a sticky hug.

Andie adored Emma, and the feelings were mutual. Their older sister Ellen, age 14, often lost patience with Emma, and brother Harry, age 12, usually overdid the "tickle monster."

Tomato sauce simmered on the stove even though dinner was two hours away. They would eat when Mr. Grove came home from his bicycle shop. Mrs. Grove was a civil engineer and worked on projects that Andie didn't understand. She left for work early in the morning when everyone was still sleeping, and she arrived home by 3:00 after picking Emma up from day care.

When Mrs. Grove got off the phone, she asked Andie if she had any homework. Andie's heart sank as she remembered the presentation. She promised her mother she would work on it later. She played outside with Emma until Harry yelled "Dinnertime!" so loudly that the whole neighborhood knew it was time for the

Grove family to eat.

"How was everybody's day?" Mr. Grove asked as he passed the bowl of spaghetti to Harry. Andie wondered why her dad didn't try to vary his questions. He always asked the same question at the beginning of every dinner. There was no way she was going to tell anyone about the adventure she had today.

"I saw Jeffrey Johnson on my way home, and he told me that Andie cried at school today!" Harry blurted.

All eyes turned to Andie. Emma said, "I can kiss you and make you better."

That stupid Jeffrey Johnson. Andie's eyes welled up with tears.

Mr. Grove said, "That boy is in my shop practically every day, including today. He didn't say anything to me." Andie was glad to hear that.

"Honey, what happened?" her mother asked gently.

"Nothing happened! I just wasn't ready to do my presentation!"

Ellen said, "You're probably going to get an 'F,'

46

you know."

Andie glared at Ellen through her tears. "Can I please be excused?"

Mrs. Grove looked at Andie's full plate of spaghetti. "Take a break and we can talk in a few minutes."

Andie left the table and went outside to the wicker rocker on the front porch. She hugged her knees and rocked as she thought about her remarkable day. The day would have been perfect if it didn't include school, or if she wasn't such a scaredy cat, or if she had a dream she could share. In one afternoon, Old Blue taught her more than she had learned in all her years of school. She wished he could be her teacher for everything. He wouldn't make her do a presentation — plus she didn't have to share him with Jeffrey Johnson. She hoped she would see Old Blue again.

Andie's mother peered out the screen door. Her daughter was smiling, and appeared to be deep in thought. Mr. and Mrs. Grove were not the type of parents who tried to shield their children from typical childhood growing pains, but it was not always clear what was "typical".

"Hey sweetie." Mrs. Grove's soft voice interrupted Andie's thoughts. "Do you want to talk about today?"

"No thanks, Mom. I'm good. But I am starving!"

Mrs. Grove smiled and opened the door for her daughter.

CHAPTER 8

Empty Nesters

"Today was a delightful day," Old Blue said to himself. Most herons do not enjoy human company, but Old Blue had lived on the Saint Jones for so long that he had grown used to their presence and had even gotten to know a few.

His life was settling back into a relaxing pace now that breeding season was over. His chicks had flown and the nest was empty. Of course, he still worried about them because most chicks do not survive past their first birthday. They are clumsy and careless which makes them easy targets for bald eagles — or even the neighborhood cat. Old Blue knew that he and his partner Harriet had done the best they could teaching their chicks about life. It was time to let go.

Old Blue and Harriet would now go their separate ways until next spring. While most herons choose new partners each year, Old Blue and Harriet had remained true to each other for many years. He loved her dearly and hated knowing that he would most likely outlive another partner, but he was hopeful that he could be with Harriet for at least a few more years.

In early spring, his courtship feathers and coloring transformed his appearance. His bill and legs turned pink, long black plumes sprang up on his head to form a crest, and long gray and black plumes appeared on his breast and back. Harriet experienced similar changes although, much to her annoyance, Old Blue's colors were brighter.

Old Blue delighted in the courtship ritual of snapping at Harriet's bill, playing hard to get. She was quite an excellent snapper herself, and she was more beautiful every year. They were a noisy but elegant couple.

Old Blue always finished the ritual by finding the perfect twig to present to Harriet which she would add to their nest. They added to the same magnificent nest year after year. It was the largest nest in the heronry, almost four feet wide and three feet deep.

After Harriet laid the eggs, Old Blue shed his crest

plumes and the plumes that lined his long neck. His bill was yellow once again and his legs and toes returned to their brownish-green shade.

He felt grateful that he and Harriet no longer had to spend every waking minute finding food for their chicks. The amount of food those small creatures consumed was astonishing. For two months, finding food for their babies was a full-time, 24-hours-a-day responsibility. While one parent remained with the chicks to keep watch against the crows and vultures who liked to steal baby herons, the other parent hunted. The goal was to catch a morsel every two minutes or so to bring back to the hungry chicks. "I am getting too old for this," he thought. Old Blue wondered how human parents had the stamina to feed children for so many years.

Of course, humans had more variety and could get their food from almost anywhere, even wrapped in plastic from a gas station. Plus, they could store it for a rainy day. They didn't have to stand still for long stretches of time waiting to nab an unsuspecting fish or mouse.

If Old Blue happened upon a turtle or snake, he was thrilled. Although they were harder to find now because of all the new houses, they were easy to catch. Fortunately, many of the new houses had fish ponds. Even though Old Blue preferred to catch fish from the bay or the river, he sometimes had no choice. He had hungry chicks to feed.

Now, however, he could sleep when and where he wished. He had only himself to feed, and he was not a picky eater. He was grateful that some conditions had improved over the past forty years or so. In the early days of industrial pollution, chemicals spread throughout the estuary, and fish ended up with these substances in their tissues. So did everyone who ate fish. The population of herons declined dramatically, hitting their lowest point in the 1960s, but since then, they had made a comeback in the region.

Old Blue remained vigilant. While he had always worried about raccoons and bald eagles lurking in the shadows, invisible enemies were a relatively new problem. Even though humans stopped using chemicals such as DDT long ago, some of those poisons still lay deep in the river's bed. Plus, humans were always experimenting with new chemicals without understanding how they might affect the environment over time. In addition, there were the occasional sewage spills, and the humans who still dumped their trash in the river.

In the time of the Lenape, children could wade in the river up to their waists and see their toes. Blue's river needed a lot of attention and care if it was ever to be that clear again. Humans had made some improvements, but like the tide, people's attention ebbed and flowed.

Diving Deeper

A rookery/heronry can vary in size from a few pairs of herons to several hundred pairs.

A female heron lays a "clutch" of two to seven eggs which incubate for almost one month. For their first two months of life, two chicks along with their two parents will consume as many calories combined per day as one human.

The young herons fly for the first time within the first two to three months of life.

DDT (dichloro-diphenyl-trichloroethane) was developed in the 1940s to kill insects that were causing malaria, typhus, and other diseases. These diseases can be deadly to human beings. In the 1950s and '60s, DDT was used on crops and in gardens as a pesticide. Wildlife that ate insects or plants with DDT were harmed. Eventually, insects became resistant to DDT, and scientists discovered that it remained in the environment and in animal and human fatty tissues. The U.S. banned its use in 1972.

CHAPTER 9

Warning!

That night, Andie dreamed she could fly. She traveled all night long next to Old Blue. She awoke the next morning with a smile and sore arms. She wondered if yesterday's adventure had been a dream. She opened the window next to her bed and stuck her head out. "Yes!" she whispered, "Summertime is coming!"

Her smile turned to a frown as she remembered the presentation.

She tiptoed around Ellen's bed, rummaged through a laundry basket to find her favorite shorts, and pulled on a red tee-shirt that matched her sneakers. Downstairs, Emma and Mr. Grove were sitting at the table eating fresh strawberries and yogurt. Harry and Ellen always slept until the last minute, but Andie savored this time with her father and Emma.

The peace and quiet ended when Harry and Ellen entered the kitchen bickering over how much time Ellen spent in the bathroom. Andie decided to leave early for school to avoid a conversation with her siblings and, hopefully, miss Jeffrey Johnson at the lockers.

"Andie!" Lily ran down the hallway to catch up to her friend. "Are you okay?"

Andie desperately wanted to tell Lily about Old Blue, but did not think Lily would believe her. Lily might think Old Blue was the imaginary friend of a childish ten-year-old. Besides, Old Blue only had room for one passenger.

"I'm fine, but I still don't have a presentation."

Lily said, "Can't you just make something up?"

Andie was surprised that Lily would make such a suggestion.

"Even if I could make something up, I just don't think I can get up there in front of everybody," Andie glumly replied.

"Andie Grove! You are one of the toughest kids I know. Of course you can do it. You'll think of something."

Andie wished she had the same confidence that

Lily had in her. She wanted to say, "Tough kids don't go crying to the nurse", but decided to change the subject.

"How's it going at your grandmother's?"

"I love my Nana, but she lives so far away that I don't get to hang out with you. The car ride to her house is so boring! I can't wait until next week when my mom finally gets home. I miss walking home with you!"

Mrs. Carlson's classroom was hot and stuffy. Nobody said a word to Andie about the previous day. She avoided making eye contact with Mrs. Carlson.

Four more students presented their dreams. Joe Murphy dreamed of going to Mars. That was pretty cool. He wore the astronaut suit he wore last Halloween. It was a little tight and too short. Jazmine Stevens dreamed of being president. She showed off a replica of the U.S. Constitution. Andie knew she would definitely vote for Jazmine when the time came. Shayna Bramson planned to be a famous singer and she sang a song. Andie thought Shayna should get extra points for singing. Jerome Parks wanted to rebuild cars. His prop was a wrench.

Andie marveled at her classmates. Why was it so hard for her and so easy for them to just march right up there and talk — or sing? They were all so amazing. Except Jeffrey Johnson.

When school finally ended, Andie stepped outside into a hot, gray, humid day. "I guess spring is over," Andie thought. She raced to Silver Lake in spite of the heat.

As she neared the lake, she heard hammering. She was sure that meant the lifeguard stand was going up. She turned the corner on Washington Street and saw a short, round man holding a sign in place while a taller man hammered the sign in place. A city pick-up truck was parked nearby.

When she got closer, she read the sign:

WARNING!

Do not consume more than one 8 oz. serving per year of fish from this lake.

"What?" she cried.

The tall man with the hammer stopped and looked at Andie.

"Why can't people fish anymore?" she asked, with a catch in her voice.

The short round man answered, "Don't worry kid, you can still fish. You just can't eat the fish." He winked at the taller man.

Andie was not amused. "Why can't people EAT the fish anymore?"

The tall man replied, "We're no scientists kiddo, but it has something to do with some kind of a chemical that has gotten into the fish."

Andie couldn't believe what she was hearing. One of her classmates, Jimmy Underwood, and his dad were always catching fish on weekends to take home to eat. And what about Old Blue? He ate a lot of fish.

She walked slowly toward the dam. A dozen geese who were exploring the grassy area near the dam stopped to let a mother duck and five ducklings march through to the river. Andie wondered how much fish the geese and ducks ate.

Then she spied a motionless heron standing at the base of the dam awaiting his prey. Was it Old Blue? Andie wanted to shout, "Don't eat the fish!"

A voice from behind her said, "We have known for some time that the river is sick."

Where did he come from? Standing right behind her on the sidewalk was Old Blue. Andie was thrilled to see her friend.

"Have you ever gotten sick?" Andie asked.

Old Blue chuckled and said, "I'm a tough old bird."

"Aren't you worried?"

The bird replied, "Always. But never mind that. Are you ready for today's journey?"

Diving Deeper

The Department of Natural Resources and Environmental Control (DNREC) started the Saint Jones River fishing warnings in 1988 due to PCB concentrations found in fish.

PCBs (polychlorinated biphenyls) are toxic, industrial chemicals that build up in the tissues of fish and other wildlife. PCBs were used to make coolants and lubricants. They were used in fluorescent lighting fixtures, electrical devices and appliances like televisions and refrigerators. These chemicals were banned in the U.S. in 1979, but they do not break down easily and may stay in the environment for years. PCBs are the main reason the warning signs about fishing went up at Silver Lake.

CHAPTER 10

The New Nation

As the pair floated above the clouds, Old Blue asked Andie if she liked history.

"I love it," she replied, "but we almost never get to study it at school. It seems like all we ever do is take tests about reading and math — and do presentations!"

"Perhaps you have noticed that I am a bit of a history connoisseur." Old Blue said. Andie had never heard that word before, but was pretty sure it meant he was an expert. She had thought it was odd that he was so fascinated with humans, but then again, why should humans be the only ones who study other animals?

"Do you know why Delaware is called 'The First State'?" Old Blue asked.

"It had something to do with either the Declaration of Independence or the Constitution. I always get those two mixed up."

Old Blue was delighted to share his knowledge. He spoke fondly of that extraordinary July day in 1776 when the Declaration of Independence was read from the porch of the courthouse in Dover. He remembered how worried he felt when he saw the troops muster on the Public Square preparing to fight in the Revolution after Delaware and the twelve other colonies separated from England. He described his relief when the thirteen newly independent states each had their own president, army, and currency—and how that lasted for more than ten years. And he recalled the thrill of witnessing the thirteen states come together to "form a more perfect union". In fact, he was perched in a tree outside the Golden Fleece Tavern on December 7, 1787, when the leaders inside decided that Delaware would be the first state to ratify the Constitution.

Andie could not believe she was learning history from someone who was there. And a bird, no less!

"Now I will show you our river. Your country is quite new. George Washington has been President for just a few months."

64

When Old Blue dipped below the clouds, Andie noticed how much more of the forest had disappeared. Then she saw a large lake that had not been there on their previous trip. "Silver Lake!" she cried. "How did it get here?"

A wooden dam was located where the concrete dam of her own time stood. A rhythmic clickety-clack sound came from the wooden building connected to the dam. Men were hurrying about the exterior of the building.

"That is a grist mill — quite a marvelous invention," Old Blue said. "They grind up wheat for flour. Delaware was known for its good wheat in this time period. The water flowing over the dam turns the water wheel, which in turn powers the millstone. This mill was also used for lumber. Instead of the water powering the millstone to grind flour, it could power a large saw to cut through logs."

Andie had never thought about why dams were built or how they worked — or that they could create a lake.

"Is the mill the reason so many more trees are gone?"

Old Blue replied, "Humans in these times believed that resources like trees would last forever, but by now, all the mature forests are gone, along with many of the animals that lived here."

"Why didn't someone stop them?"

"Humans believed the land was theirs to do with as they pleased. There were not many laws to protect the environment. They thought that being free to do whatever they wanted was more important than caring for trees and the environment."

Andie wondered if the people who cared about this kind of freedom were the same ones who thought enslaving other people was a good idea.

She turned her attention back to the lake.

"Is the lake called 'Silver Lake'?"

"In these days, they called the lake 'Mill Lake'."

Andie thought that wasn't a very creative name. But then again, neither was "Silver."

"Humans can be excellent problem solvers even if they aren't always creative with their names," Old Blue said.

The two friends circled the lake once more before heading toward the Public Square. The building Andie knew as the Old State House had just been built, and several other buildings had been added since their last visit. Christ Church looked brand new.

The river was narrower than their last visit, but still much wider than in her time. She had never seen a boat bigger than a kayak on the river, but a large boat with two masts sat anchored as two men threw items overboard.

"Why are they littering?" Andie cried out.

"They are getting rid of their ballast — probably rocks — to make the ship lighter so that it doesn't get stuck in the riverbed," Old Blue replied.

He explained how boats often needed to weigh themselves down with heavy materials so that they would not tip over. "The problem now — in 1789 — is the river has become shallower. Soil that used to be held in place by tree roots is washed into the river every time it rains."

Andie wondered how Old Blue could possibly think humans were good problem solvers.

Diving Deeper

All of Delaware's lakes and ponds were created by humans. Most of the larger ponds and lakes were created by damming the flow of a stream in order to harness the water to operate mills.

CHAPTER 11

Shallops and Storms

Old Blue continued his course along the river toward the Delaware Bay. Several large plantations and many small farms had shown up since their last visit.

Thin ribbons of smoke trickled from many of the chimneys. "Why would people light a fire on such a hot and humid day?" asked Andie.

"They are cooking," Old Blue replied.

The river was busy with many different kinds of large and small boats. The biggest boat looked like the one Andie had just seen near the Public Square.

"That is a shallop," Old Blue informed her. "Shallops were good boats for navigating the river and its tributaries. That one looks like it is filled with cabbage and asparagus. It is probably heading out to the Delaware Bay, up to Philadelphia on the Delaware River. That boat could probably carry a dozen humans if it weren't carrying all that produce."

Andie remarked, "The river really was like a highway, wasn't it?"

Several small rowboats were anchored while their passengers fished. One of the men reeled in a squirming fish and exclaimed, "It is a good day for trout!" Old Blue eyed the catch hungrily.

Three longer, wider boats floated leisurely along. Each one carried several fishermen. Old Blue said the boats were called "dories". The men in these boats were also having good luck catching fish. "Fish were plentiful in these times. And the oysters! Plump, juicy and abundant! Humans ate oysters at every meal!"

Andie suddenly noticed how quiet everything was, even though the fields and river were filled with people. No motors, just the sound of the breeze and conversation. The quiet did not last. As they turned the bend, they heard sawing and hammering. Several buildings appeared. "That is a shipyard. A lot of large boats were built here. I am getting quite ahead of myself, but by the 1860s, shipbuilding was the second largest industry in Delaware — second to flour milling."

They coasted in silence until they came to the mouth of the river at Bowers Beach. A shallop had just entered the bay, and at least twenty boats were anchored near the beach. "Crabs and scallops!" Old Blue said enthusiastically.

Andie was starting to feel a little hungry herself.

Suddenly, the wind began to blow and the sky darkened. The sailors in the shallop swiftly rolled up the sails. A black cloud from the east accompanied by flashes of lightening moved rapidly toward them.

"I had better get you to a shelter other than a tree top," Old Blue said. He knew the typical mid-Atlantic thunderstorm would hit hard and end quickly. He descended onto the edge of a field where he spied an open barn door. A small brown horse stood inside, lazily chewing hay. The horse did not seem bothered by the approaching storm or his visitors.

"Stay here and I will return as soon as the lightning stops."

Before Andie could protest, Old Blue was in flight. She looked at her watch, but once again, it had stopped at 3:20.

The barn grew dark and the rumblings were now directly overhead. The horse stopped eating, lifted his head and gazed directly at Andie. "Can you see me?" Andie whispered. Lightning lit up the barn. Deafening thunder immediately followed. The horse began to pace.

Normally Andie loved rainstorms. Her mom, who was always busy, would stop whatever she was doing and get everyone to sit on the front porch to "enjoy the show". If it was a thunderstorm, however, they would watch it from inside, because Andie's mom said it was too dangerous to be outside. Andie wondered what the weather was like at home right now.

BAM! Another clap of thunder as loud as the last one. Both Andie and the horse jumped. Rain pounded the leaky roof. Andie moved to the corner where she sat on a damp bale of hay. She shivered. The horse stood alert, awaiting the next clap of thunder.

Within a few minutes, the darkness lifted as the rain slowed. The time between lightning strikes and thunder claps grew longer and the noise more distant. Old Blue's head appeared around the barn door.

"Danger is over!" he announced as he strolled in. The outline of a fish was noticeable in his long neck. The horse returned to his hay.

The rain drops grew lighter now as hints of sunshine glowed around the gray clouds.

"Let me show you what the next century looked like. Hop on!"

Diving Deeper

Lightning can strike anywhere outdoors and is attracted to the tallest structure such as a tree or flagpole. If you are standing near a tree or flagpole when lightning strikes, the current from the lightning can travel down the item and "jump" toward you. The safest place to be is inside a house — but there are still risks inside. A lightning charge can travel through wiring and pipes in a house, so it is important to avoid activities such as taking a shower or bath (or anything dealing with running water), typing on a computer, playing video games, talking on a landline (or doing anything that involves contact with something that is plugged in). Wireless devices are safe to use. Shoes should be worn when walking on soil or a wet/damp floor.

Most large buildings are built with lightning protection systems, that might include a lightning rod (a Benjamin Franklin invention). If lightning strikes a lightning rod, the lightning charge gets conducted to the ground through a wire.

CHAPTER 12

Human Ingenuity

Andie marveled at how the sky could be so gray below the clouds, while at the same time, so blue above. Light rain was still falling when she and Old Blue descended from the clouds. Old Blue remained high in the sky so that Andie could take in the most recent changes to the landscape, which included more houses, buildings, roads, and carriages, but fewer trees and a browner river.

In the distance, a train chugged along, steam billowing from its stack. Blue explained, "That is the Philadelphia, Wilmington, and Baltimore Railroad. Another example of human ingenuity. It was built just a few years ago. Fortunately, humans had the good sense to build most of it on sturdy ground."

Andie said, "The whole place looks so different from just a few minutes ago!"

Old Blue replied, "Actually, our last visit was 70 years ago."

He continued, "The railroad made it easier to transport more lumber. The economy was booming. Farmers switched from growing grain to growing fruits and vegetables because cheaper fertilizers were easy to get. This led to the canning industry, and for a while, Dover was a leader in this industry."

Andie felt a twinge of pride. A lot of important history had happened in her hometown.

So much had changed over the last 70 years. "What are those buildings over there near the mill?"

"The new building closest to the flour mill is a saw mill. The buildings a little closer to us belong to a tannery. That is where they make leather — a dirty and smelly process."

"Is that why the river is so brown?" Andie asked.

"Yes, although Dover wasn't the only town that used the river in this way. If we fly back toward the source of the river, you will see more mills."

Old Blue descended until he was gliding along the tree tops. Light rain continued to fall. Andie saw a group of horses and cows standing neck deep in the river. "Are they swimming?" she asked.

"No, they are trying to escape the mosquitoes."

Andie thought about how her parents were always trying to come up with new ways to fight mosquitoes. They had recently put up two bat houses but no bats had moved in yet.

"Mosquitoes breed in wetlands. Delaware has always had a considerably high number of mosquitoes. Let your parents know that the more birds they can attract to their property, the fewer mosquitoes they will have."

Andie wondered if there was anything that Old Blue did not know. She wished she could bring him to school to help her with her presentation.

"We have covered a lot of years and topics today," Old Blue said.

Andie had to admit she felt pretty tired and overwhelmed. When they returned to the Silver Lake playground, the sky was still gray and light rain was still falling. Andie's watch resumed ticking.

Diving Deeper

Turning an animal hide into a soft piece of leather requires very hazardous chemicals to remove the hair and make the leather flexible. Tanneries used to dump hair and other waste products into the waterways. High tides would push the contaminated waste inland. Today, tanneries are strictly regulated in most developed countries.

Mosquitoes lay their eggs wherever they find standing water: flower pots, birdbaths, garbage cans, clogged rain gutters, etc. The eggs take about three days to hatch into larvae and then about 12 days to grow into adults who can fly away.

CHAPTER 13

Civil War

Old Blue felt great affection for his young friend as he watched Andie half skip, half run home. He recalled how once upon a time he had the same youthful energy. He enjoyed this time with his new friend and wished he could show her so much more of Dover's history, but he had to pick his visits carefully as their time together was limited.

Old Blue knew he would not bring Andie back to the Civil War. Even though no battles took place in Delaware, intense disagreements drove families apart and violent clashes between neighbors occasionally broke out in all three counties. In Dover, most young men fought for the Union, but some joined the Confederacy. Many died.

The Saint Jones River was dramatically affected by the war. The saw mill on Silver Lake — which was called "Shakespeare's Mill Pond" in those days —

specialized in oak shipbuilding timber. The mill never produced so much timber as it did during the Civil War. In fact, Shakespeare's Mill was one of the most important east coast timber manufacturers that supplied lumber to the Union Army.

If Old Blue had brought Andie back, she would have seen more shipyards and sawmills along the river. Out on the bay, Andie would have watched many ships crowded with soldiers and weapons heading north and a few heading south.

Although the Civil War was an important period in the life of the Saint Jones River, Old Blue decided that ten-year-old Andie could wait a few years to learn about war.

Diving Deeper

The Civil War had many causes, but most historians agree that the root cause was slavery. After the war ended in 1865, the 13th amendment was added to the Constitution officially ending slavery.

CHAPTER 14

"I'm Thirsty!"

That evening, Ellen was in charge of babysitting while Mr. and Mrs. Grove attended a community meeting. Of course, Andie and Harry didn't need a sitter, but that didn't stop Ellen from trying to boss them around. Ellen told Andie to take care of Emma. Andie didn't mind. She adored Emma and she didn't have any homework, except for the presentation. She still had no ideas.

Ellen shut herself in their bedroom to talk on her phone. Harry watched TV. Andie played hide and seek with Emma. Emma never looked for a place to hide until Andie called out "Ready or not, here I come!" Her hiding places were always nearby and easy to find. If her loud breathing didn't give it away, her giggles usually did.

"I'm thirsty!" Emma announced when she grew tired of the game. She pulled her step-stool to the sink, took one of her sippy cups from the drainer and filled it with water. Andie suddenly felt sad.

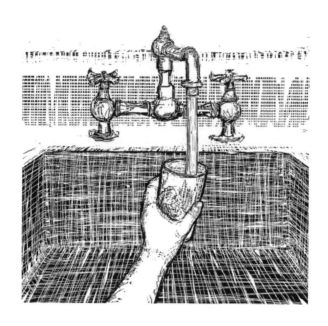

"What's wrong with you?" Ellen asked as she entered the kitchen to get an apple.

Andie paused before answering. Sometimes it was risky sharing with Ellen.

"Do you know that people are not allowed to eat fish from Silver Lake any more?" Andie said.

"So? It's not like we eat fish from Silver Lake!" Ellen replied.

"I'm worried about Emma's future." Andie responded quietly.

86

"Geez Andie, you sound like you are so old," Ellen said. "If you are so worried, do something about it!" Then Ellen returned to her phone.

As Andie was helping Emma get ready for bed, Ellen's words kept echoing through her mind. What could she possibly do? She was just a kid — a kid who was afraid to do a 5th grade presentation.

Diving Deeper

Tap water comes from ground water (underground streams and aquifers), streams, rivers, and lakes. Most people in the U.S. get their drinking water from a public water system. Federal law (the Safe Drinking Water Act) requires that cities test public water at regular intervals to make sure the water meets certain standards of quality. People who get their water from private wells are responsible for testing their own water. There have been cases when city or local governments have not done a good job testing their water quality. People can become very ill from drinking water that does not meet federal standards.

CHAPTER 15

Stormy Wednesday

Rain pounded the Groves' old house throughout the night. Andie awoke to a thunderstorm. Her first thought was of Old Blue. She wondered   where he went during thunderstorms.

By the time breakfast was over, the thunder was gone but the rain persisted. Mr. Grove looked out the kitchen window and shook his head saying, "It's going to be a wet one and that means business will be slow. I guess I'll be driving you to school today. If it is still raining like this at the end of the day, either your mother or I will get you after school." Andie hoped the rain would stop.

The day proceeded slowly. Rain was still coming down as students began their presentations in Mrs. Carlson's class. Zachary Garner's dream was to be a professional basketball player and his prop was, of course, a basketball. Zach was the second shortest kid in the class, next to Andie. His presentation was also short.

Jayla Manning's dream was to run a business and get rich. She didn't have any idea about what kind of business. Her prop was a wad of monopoly money.

Andie thought the presentations were becoming less creative. Then she remembered that she didn't even have an idea.

The last presenter for the day was Jimmy Underwood, the boy who liked to fish with his father at Silver Lake. He told the class he was going to own his own boat someday and make his living as a fisherman. He described how happy he felt when he was fishing and how cool it was to be able to eat what you caught yourself. His prop was an old yellowed newspaper picture that showed him and his dad holding a big fish.

Andie felt sick. She doubted Jimmy had seen the new sign about fishing. She wondered if she should say something to him. Would she be saving his life or ruining his dream? She decided she would say something — but not yet.

The first bell interrupted her thoughts. As the bus

riders filed out of the classroom, Mrs. Carlson called Andie to her desk. Lily looked up from the homework she had already begun. Jeffrey Johnson leaned forward to eavesdrop. Andie swallowed hard and walked slowly to Mrs. Carlson's desk.

"Have you come up with any ideas yet for your presentation?" Mrs. Carlson asked quietly.

Andie looked at Mrs. Carlson and shrugged. "I just don't know what I want to be when I grow up."

Andie felt Lily and Jeffrey watching her. She could hear the rain lashing against the classroom windows. Just then, the second bell rang. Jeffrey bolted out of the door while Lily gathered her papers. Andie turned and gave Lily a weak wave, signaling to Lily to go on without her.

Mrs. Carlson smiled kindly at Andie. "Most people don't know what they want to be when they grow up. Many grownups aren't even sure! Think bigger if you want. Any dream will work for this assignment. The point, really, is to give you practice with public speaking. You can even make something up if you'd like."

That was what Lily had said.

Andie thanked Mrs. Carlson and promised she would come up with something. She walked out of the front entrance and was blinded by flashing headlights. She wondered how long her mother had been waiting.

That evening, Andie felt like drawing. She tried to draw Old Blue, but she had his knees backwards, and he resembled a giraffe with wings. She looked up some pictures of great blue herons on the computer and found one that came close. She copied it carefully and added Old Blue's bald spot.

The rain continued through the night.

Diving Deeper

A heron's "backward knees" are not knees, but more like our ankles. Their knees are hidden under their feathers.

Herons have special feathers on their chest that fray and become powdery. Using their toes, herons comb the powder over other areas of their body in order to keep their feathers clean and waterproof.

92

CHAPTER 16

Running Out of Time

When Andie awoke on Thursday morning, she listened carefully. The busy street sounded wet. A bird was singing. She peered through the blinds on her window. Lingering raindrops clung to the screen. The sky was gray.

At school, students were restless. Summer was only two and a half weeks away. Except for a few final tests and quizzes, most students were done with schoolwork. Not Andie. She still had no ideas for the dreaded presentation. She couldn't even make one up. Her mind kept drifting from the feeling of flying through the air on Old Blue's back to the thrill of jumping into Silver Lake as soon as the beach opened.

In Mrs. Carlson's class, Andie gazed anxiously out the window. The sky was still overcast, but no rain. She hoped Old Blue would be waiting for her today.

Andie counted nine students, including herself, who had not yet presented. When Mrs. Carlson asked for volunteers, three hands went up. Mrs. Carlson said, "My dears, please remember that Tuesday is the last possible day for presentations. Monday is Memorial Day. I must have four volunteers tomorrow, or I will need to volunteer you."

CHAPTER 17

Transportation Revolution

Andie was shocked when she saw the lake after school. Water surged over the dam, breaching the banks. The entire picnic area was under water. Huge puddles and broken branches covered the playground.

"Storms didn't have this effect years ago."

Andie had grown used to Old Blue's sudden appearances, but she was surprised by his statement. "You didn't have big storms long ago?" she asked.

Old Blue assured her there had always been violent and unexpected storms, but there were more wetlands back then. "The marshes were like sponges soaking up excess water, but as the marshes were filled in to make room for more farmland and buildings, the water had to go somewhere."

Andie studied the scene. It looked like one of

those disasters on the news. How long would it be until the park and the lake returned to normal? As soon as school ended tomorrow, Memorial Day weekend would begin.

"Can we go see what it looks like further down the river?" she asked.

The two travelers flew along the river surveying the damage. The water lapped at the edge of the sidewalk along Kings Highway where a man in a bucket truck was trimming a damaged tree. He did not notice Andie and Old Blue. The patio at Fraizer's Restaurant was under water. A large red umbrella dangled from some loose branches in a holly tree beside the Loockerman Street bridge.

Water rushed under the bridge as Andie and Old Blue flew over. A rusty supermarket cart lay along the banks of the river on the other side of the bridge. Andie watched the current pull branches and twigs, trapping them in tall grass with each turn. The river's narrow twists and turns gradually widened as Andie and Old Blue left the city limits.

They passed over three small boats. Two were

motoring along. Andie thought they were crazy to be boating with the river so wild. The third boat held two men and was anchored next to tall grasses. One of the men pulled a cage up from the water, while the second man sat holding a fishing pole. Andie wondered if they knew about the fish warnings.

Up into the clouds, Old Blue flew. The gray clouds blended so completely with the gray sky that Andie didn't know they were in a cloud until she could no longer see anything at all.

"Next stop, 1887 — almost thirty years later than yesterday!" Old Blue announced, sounding like a train conductor.

When they exited below the clouds, Andie saw large patches of green leaves blanketing the river. "Are those lily pads?" she asked.

"Lotus lilies. They were probably brought here from China or Japan. Humans have a habit of bringing new species to places where they don't belong."

Andie thought they looked pretty and wondered why they no longer existed in her time.

As Old Blue flew toward The Green, he described

how people regularly widened and deepened the river to make it easier for bigger boats to travel up the river. "Unfortunately, it also made it easier for salt water to travel up the river from the bay. Salt water killed a lot of the native grasses and probably killed the lotus lilies too. All that beach grass that you currently see, is called 'phragmites.' It is not a native grass, but it loves the salt water."

As Andie shifted her gaze away from the lotus lilies, she was astonished to see a crowd of people with luggage standing on a large dock behind The Green. A large steamboat was chugging toward the landing.

"That boat is so cool!" Andie exclaimed.

"Yes." Old Blue agreed. "Those steamships were something to see! Red-carpeted dining rooms, entertainment, three decks, enough room for 200 humans. They came to Dover about three times a week, steaming in with the earliest high tide of the day and leaving in the middle of the day, at the second high tide. It took them about eight and a half hours to get to Philadelphia."

"I wish we still had a dock in Dover! And steamships!"

"Steamships stopped coming to downtown

Dover after a few years because the river needed constant dredging due to all the silt. In fact, it wasn't long before trains replaced the steamships."

As if on cue, a train whistle blew. Old Blue flew in its direction, toward the downtown area. "The refrigerated railroad car has been around for about twenty years by now. That meant that more goods could be transported further. Dozens of freight trains came through Dover every day. That one there, though, is a passenger train heading up to Philadelphia."

The elegant brick train station stood at the end of

Loockerman Street — which was still a dirt road. The street was lined with businesses, hitching posts, horses and wagons. The sidewalks were filled with shoppers. A group of children stood outside an ice cream store, enjoying their treat. One of them gazed up at Andie and smiled.

Women's dresses were still fitted and long, but no longer wide at the hem. Their hats, however, were quite wide. One woman gazed at her reflection in a store window and adjusted her large feathered hat. Andie giggled. "That is the silliest hat I have ever seen!"

"In these times," Old Blue said, "I had to be especially careful. Hat makers loved to use our feathers, and as a result, the Great Blue Heron population began to decline."

Andie felt terrible for laughing. These hats were literally a matter of life and death for Old Blue. "When do cars come along?" she asked, changing the subject.

Old Blue answered, "Cars have just been invented. In about twenty years, a wealthy Delawarean named Thomas Coleman DuPont will offer to pay for a highway which will connect the three counties. A few years after that, cars will be mass produced by Henry Ford."

As Old Blue soared higher, Andie noticed more

changes in the landscape below. "Are those peach or-chards?" she asked. The annual peach festival was one of her favorite events.

"Peach and apple orchards. Around this time, Kent County was considered by many to be the apple capital of the country. And see over there? If I brought you closer, you would see acres and acres of tomato seedlings. Delaware also provided the whole country with canned tomatoes."

Andie scanned the landscape and saw that many dirt roads now criss-crossed the area. A number of horse-drawn wagons meandered along the roads. It was hard for Andie to imagine that these wagons would soon be replaced by cars. Then she thought about the Amish people in her town who still drove horse-drawn buggies.

"Are the Amish people here yet?" she asked.

"Not yet," Old Blue answered. "They will begin to arrive in 1915, attracted by all the available inexpen-sive land."

Andie wondered if the Amish lifestyle looked as out of place in 1915 as it did in her time. She was astonished by the historical changes she had witnessed this afternoon, even though she knew changes would dramatically speed up in the 20th century. She was curious how the Amish were able to maintain such simple lives in the midst of so much change. She also wondered if Amish children had to do presentations.

Diving Deeper

Although a native phragmites exists, it has been largely replaced by a non-native, invasive phragmites which thrives where wetlands and rivers are disturbed through ditching and straightening. Various unsuccessful attempts have been made to get rid of this invasive phragmites, but scientists have recently determined that the non-native phragmites might be useful, because its thick root system seems to protect against erosion.

CHAPTER 18

Not Dinner Talk

Mrs. Grove had to work late which meant Mr. Grove closed his shop early to take care of Emma and dinner. The family was about to sit down to eat when Mrs. Grove came through the door.

"What a day!" Mrs. Grove exclaimed. "Every time we get a storm like that, we get a million calls about roads, bridges and sewage."

"Sewage? You mean poo?" Harry asked, knowing exactly what his mother was talking about.

"Harry! That is not dinner talk!" Ellen scolded.

"Mom started it!" Harry retorted.

Andie asked how the storm caused sewage problems.

"Ewww! Do we really need to talk about this?" Ellen whined.

Mrs. Grove ignored Ellen and explained, "The

water treatment plants that treat the sewage do a great job, but the city's pipes are old and have some cracks. That means that sometimes the sewage leaks out of the pipes or the excess rain enters into the pipes which forces the treatment plant to have to work extra hard. When the system gets overwhelmed, it cannot handle the extra volume and sometimes breaks down."

"Does the sewage ever get into the Saint Jones River?" Andie asked.

"Unfortunately, the poor Saint Jones seems to suffer more than most rivers in the state," her mother answered. "But we are still better off today than a hundred years ago. People used to send sewage directly into rivers and oceans without any treatment. The state used to have to ban oyster harvesting every now and then because the pollution was so bad."

Ellen interrupted her mother. "Do we really have to talk about this at dinner?"

Mrs. Grove continued, "Sometimes the state still has to ban oyster harvesting if there is a big spill. But when everything goes according to plan—which is most

106

of the time—today's treatment plants do an amazing job. You would never know that the water had been dirty."

Andie was skeptical, but decided to bring a new fact into the conversation. "You know, one hundred years ago, strong storms didn't cause nearly as much flooding as they do today—at least not around here."

Mr. Grove asked, "Did you learn that in Mrs. Carlson's class?"

Andie paused before answering. "No, I learned it from someone at the lake today."

Andie's parents looked at each other. Her mother said, "I appreciate how much you love that lake, but I do not want you going there by yourself. And you know better than to talk to strangers!"

"I am not alone! The place is filled with birds, fish, squirrels, and great blue herons. Not to mention children, moms, dads and babysitters."

Andie's parents exchanged another look.

Ellen rolled her eyes. "Honestly Andie, you are so weird! Mom, can I please be excused?"

Diving Deeper

Cities and towns have sewer systems where waste travels through pipes and pumping systems to wastewater treatment plants. There, the solids and sludge are removed and the water is disinfected and cleaned. The water is then discharged back into the environment.

Rural areas often use septic systems where a tank on a personal property collects all the sewage (wastewater). The solids in the sewage settle to the bottom while the liquid drains into a "leach field" where it is treated by the soil where bacteria breaks everything down.

Many cities do not have adequate sewage treatment plants and the sewage gets dumped into rivers and lakes.

Some cities have separate tanks for storm water so that sewage treatment plants do not get overwhelmed.

CHAPTER 19

Finally Friday

Sunshine flooded Andie's room, waking her up before her alarm went off. She jumped out of bed when she remembered that the end of today's school day was the start of the Memorial Day weekend and the unofficial beginning of summer. Cars would jam roads from the north and the west on their way to the beaches. Grills would roll out of garages where they had been hibernating for the winter and the smell of hotdogs and hamburgers would fill the air. If only the presentation was done!

On her way to school, the only evidence that there had been a storm were the puddles around the leaf-clogged storm drains. Andie thought about the many things she had learned in the last few days. Maybe she could present something she learned from Old Blue. What would she say if Mrs. Carlson asked about her sources? Maybe she could teach them about sewage.

They should learn about that. "Really?" she said to herself. "Everyone is sharing their dream career, and I'm going to share about sewage?" She tried to imagine how Jeffrey Johnson would react. It wasn't hard.

Morning classes were dull. The teachers seemed less creative now that the school year was coming to a close. Andie didn't mind doing crossword puzzles and word searches, but in every class? Every class except Mrs. Carlson's.

As the clock ticked closer to 3:00, Andie's excitement about the weekend grew but so did her anxiety about the presentation. Fortunately, four students volunteered to do their presentations, leaving only Andie and Donald Jones for Tuesday. Andie envied all of her classmates who had completed their work, but she wasn't going to let jealousy stop her from enjoying her three-day weekend.

By now, the class had grown weary listening to presentations, and Mrs. Carlson worked hard to keep students quiet and focused. "Do I need to make a new seating chart?" she threatened. Her warning worked for the first two presentations.

Scotty Steele wanted to be a surgeon. He showed a gross photograph of open-heart surgery. Annie Edwards was going to join the Air Force and gave each student a tiny American flag. She reminded everyone that Memorial Day was not for picnics, but to honor those who had died for our country.

Jeffrey Johnson started snapping his gum during Marsha O'Malley's presentation about quilting. Mrs. Carlson moved his seat next to her desk. Poor Peter Jackson was stuck presenting last. He stammered a lot and was not very well prepared. He was explaining how to carve decoy ducks when the first bell rang. Students leapt out of their chairs, but Mrs. Carlson called out in a loud, firm voice, "Sit down unless you would like to spend Tuesday after school with me!"

Everyone sat down. She asked Peter to try to sum up the rest of his information in 30 seconds or less. He did it in 20 seconds. "Have a safe and happy weekend!" Mrs. Carlson said as she dismissed the bus riders.

While the walkers waited for their bell, Mrs.

Carlson approached Andie. "Are you doing okay? Have you come up with an idea yet?" Mrs. Carlson asked.

Andie nodded slowly. She had ideas — just no good ones.

"Will you be ready to present on Tuesday?"

Andie was pretty sure she had no choice. "Yes," she answered.

The walkers' bell rang. Andie hurried off to the lake.

CHAPTER 20

Growing Pains

The sky was blue and cloudless. Water roared loudly as it tumbled over the dam, but the river had receded back to its banks. Two city workers wearing yellow reflective vests were picking up storm debris. One of the pavilions was decorated for a party.

Andie was surprised the city workers had not yet weeded the beach or set up the lifeguard stand. Maybe they would work overtime. She felt bad for anyone who had to work on this magnificent weekend. Then she remembered that her father always worked Memorial Day weekend. This weekend was like Christmas for him. Everyone discovered they needed a new bike or a tune up when Memorial Day rolled around.

Two boys were playing catch on the muddy field next to the playground, but the playground itself was surprisingly empty. Andie walked toward the swing-set thinking she would swing while she waited for Old Blue to show up.

"There is no time for that!"

Old Blue was perched on top of the yellow slide. "Climb aboard! We have much to see."

The cloudless sky allowed Andie to watch the landscape change as Old Blue flew back in time. It was like watching a movie play backwards. Houses disappeared development by development. Parking lots and roads receded from view as trees took their places. The massive Dover Air Force Base shrunk and then disappeared entirely, replaced by farms and one small road.

Old Blue said, "Now I am going to switch directions and move forward about twenty years."

Andie watched as three farms quickly turned into a small airport with one runway. The single runway then became three runways. Soon, several taxiways, a large parking lot, and a control tower were added. Small planes with propellers on their noses lined up in a neat row on the field. They reminded her of the planes called "crop dusters" that she often saw during the summer, spraying crops with different kinds of chemicals.

Next, hundreds more acres of land disappeared, replaced by more runways, a larger control tower, a huge steel hangar, and planes that looked like the bombers she saw in some of the World War II movies her parents liked to watch.

Suddenly, the air base looked like a city. Schools, a nine-hole golf course, more hangars, longer runways, and massive planes with bright orange noses filled the fields. Hundreds of houses and dozens of shopping centers bordered the base. Thousands of cars crowded the new wide roads.

Andie was shocked by the rapid and dramatic changes that Dover Air Force Base brought to the landscape.

Old Blue began his lesson. "Although Dover's most historic contribution was its role in the ratification of the Constitution, the average person knows about Dover because of the air force base. The first airfield was built in the 1930s when many nations became concerned about what was going on in Germany. The U.S. government hoped the airfield would never have to be used,

115

but then World War II happened."

Andie had not learned about the World Wars in school yet. Old Blue added, "The air base is the reason the population here grew so quickly. Imagine what kind of effect all these additional humans and new houses had on the river."

Andie was puzzled. There were barely any boats on the river. Cars had obviously replaced boats. Why would more people and houses affect the river? Then she remembered the previous night's dinner conversation.

As Old Blue rounded the curve near the John Dickinson mansion, Andie gasped. Tires drifted along the river. Large rusty containers were piled high along the shore, dark liquid oozing from them. A mountain of old couches, wrecked cars, tattered clothes, broken bottles, and other trash spread along the river and back into the marshes for acres and acres.

Old Blue said, "Humans everywhere have always dumped garbage into waterways. More humans has always meant more garbage. Around here, this is one of the places where they used to dump it. Imagine what you would see in your day if humans still brought all their trash to the river."

Andie was stunned. "People are disgusting!" she cried.

"No," Old Blue replied, "Humans are human. And they learn slowly sometimes. But they do learn. This dump no longer exists in your time. It was cleaned up some time ago and the river gets monitored regularly. Many excellent human ideas and actions are really helping. Laws have been passed to protect animals and the environment."

Choking through tears, Andie said, "But now people can't even eat the fish from the river, so it doesn't sound like it's any better!"

Old Blue was quiet for a moment. "Yes, great damage has been done which scientists are still learning about. Each generation of children will need to be taught how to properly care for the environment. Your river will always need someone like you."

Diving Deeper

People have always generated trash, but as cities developed, so did ways to manage trash. Most cities provide garbage collection services which transport the garbage to landfills where it is either burned or buried.

In rural communities, people either pay a private contractor or they transport their own trash to dumps or landfills.

The average person generates between two and three pounds of garbage per day. Much of this waste can be either recycled or composted.

Before plastic was developed, materials such as wood, glass, metal, and clay were used for daily items. By the 1950s, plastic had replaced many traditional materials — especially in wealthy countries. Plastic is cheap, lightweight, and versatile. It is used in packaging, automobiles, furniture, toys, disposable diapers, construction, and more. Unfortunately, plastic does not biodegrade. Much of it ends up in landfills and waterways. Approximately nine billion tons of plastic have been created since the 1950s. According to the United States Environmental Protection Agency, in 2015 alone, over 26 million tons of plastic ended up in U.S. landfills.

CHAPTER 21

Closed Until Further Notice

"Your river will always need someone like you." Old Blue's words echoed through Andie's mind when she awoke the next morning. What could she possibly do? Everyone already knew that littering was bad. She was feeling overwhelmed and depressed until she realized what day it was.

She quickly found her bathing suit at the bottom of her tee-shirt drawer and dug her old flip-flops out of the closet. She was pleased to see she had slightly out-grown last year's beach attire. She threw shorts and a tee-shirt over her suit and ran down the stairs. Her mother was sipping coffee as she watched Emma work on a puzzle.

"I'm going swimming!" Andie exclaimed happily.

"Breakfast and sunscreen first young lady — and

only if the lifeguard is on duty."

Andie opened the refrigerator and grabbed an apple. "Got it! Thanks Mom. I'll be back in a couple of hours!"

"Sunscreen!" Mrs. Grove said sternly as she retrieved a tube of lotion from the cabinet over the sink. She applied the sunscreen to Andie's face and back while Andie slathered it on her arms and legs. "It is only 10:00, so if the lifeguard isn't there yet, I want you to come home and then we can all go back after lunch."

Andie ran out letting the screen door slam behind her. She rounded the corner on Washington Street, expecting to see a crowded beach, but only a handful of cars were in the parking lot. The beach was empty.

Was she too early? When Andie got closer to the entrance, her heart sank. There was no lifeguard stand, and the beach was still covered with weeds. Then she saw the new sign tacked above the fish warning sign.

Beach closed until further notice.
No Swimming Allowed.

Andie stared at the sign, certain there was some mistake. She could not catch her breath. She felt like she had been kicked in the stomach. She sat on the grass and as she began to sob, Old Blue landed at her feet.

Andie cried, "I thought you said the water was cleaner now!"

Old Blue responded gently, "In some ways, it is. You don't see couches and tires floating down the river anymore. Humans are more careful with their trash. The harm is less visible and less obvious now."

Andie kept weeping. Old Blue's information did not make her feel any better.

He continued, "Humans still don't understand that every time it rains, poison is washed into the river."

"Poison?" Andie sobbed in horror. "What do you mean 'poison?'"

Andie's tears subsided as Old Blue explained what he meant. She listened carefully. Then she got an idea.

Diving Deeper

The City of Dover bought the lake and mill site at Silver Lake in March 1938, so that citizens would have a public space for boating, waterskiing, fishing, swimming, and picnicking.

CHAPTER 22

A Plan

Andie trudged home slowly, thoughts swirling through her head. She felt sad and angry, but also determined. When she entered her house, her mother was still drinking coffee and watching Emma, who had switched to Legos. "Not open yet?" Mrs. Grove said without turning around.

"Not open ever!" Andie cried.

Mrs. Grove sighed. For years, there had been rumors that Silver Lake beach was going to close. One of the neighbors had even mentioned it at the community meeting they attended earlier in the week. She was annoyed that the neighborhood had not been officially informed.

As her mother held her close, Andie's sobs gradually grew quieter. After a couple of minutes, she pulled herself away from her mother and wiped her tears away. "Do we have any poster board lying around?" she asked.

Mrs. Grove was surprised and relieved by how quickly her daughter recovered. Andie disappeared into her room for the rest of the weekend, only coming out to eat. She would not even come to the phone when Lily called. Ellen complained to her mother that Andie was hogging the bedroom, but left her alone when she saw what her sister was doing.

Diving Deeper

In 2008, the City of Dover decided to close Silver Lake to swimming due to the increasing frequency of high bacteria levels and algal blooms which can cause respiratory problems in people.

CHAPTER 23

The River Guardian

Andie took three deep, slow breaths as she made her way to the front of the classroom. She hadn't dressed up. Her hair was even more disheveled than usual. Her props were two wrinkled posters. Mrs. Carlson looked concerned.

Andie began, "I don't know what I want to be when I grow up, but I do have a dream."

She unrolled her first poster. Her hands were shaking. "This is my friend Old Blue. He has taught me that humans can make a terrible mess of things. But he also taught me that we can be very smart and creative."

Someone giggled. Jeffrey Johnson folded his hands over his chest and smirked.

Andie unrolled her other poster which had a thick black line drawn across the middle. Above the line, she had carefully written in big black letters, "Beach closed until further notice. No Swimming Allowed." Below the line, she wrote "WARNING! Do not consume more than one 8 oz. serving per year of fish from this lake."

Andie continued. "We need clean water. Old Blue needs clean water. All the fish and animals need it too. I learned in the last few days that the river and lake have been sick for a long time. People have changed their ways as they have learned how their actions affect the water. We don't try to straighten rivers anymore, or destroy marshes so that we can put buildings on them, or dump tires and furniture in the river, but we do still dump sewage and poisonous chemicals into the river.

Most people don't even know they are doing it."

By this time, Andie's hands had stopped shaking. She looked around at her classmates. They were all listening. Lily gave her a thumbs up sign. Jeffrey Johnson had unfolded his arms and was leaning forward attentively. Mrs. Carlson was smiling.

"When it rains, the fertilizers our parents put on their lawns to make the grass pretty plus the pesticides and herbicides they use on their flowers and vegetables in their gardens get washed into the river. The same thing happens on farms. All this stuff might be okay in gardens and farms, but when it runs into the river or seeps into the ground, it is poison. It causes algae to grow in the rivers and lakes which means there is less oxygen for the fish, so the fish suffocate and die. Plus, these algae blooms make the water poisonous. The problem is the worst when there is too much rain or when it is really hot outside for a long time."

Andie wondered if she was getting too technical with her information, but everyone looked like they were still paying attention. "Nature is good about keeping everything in balance but these chemicals are so harmful that nature can't fix it. Now we aren't allowed to eat the fish or swim in the lake anymore. I don't think people mean to be mean. I think they just don't know."

Andie paused and took another deep breath. "My dream is that Silver Lake will be open for swimming by next Memorial Day and that people and the herons of the Saint Jones can eat as much fish as they want. I don't know how to fix it, and I know we aren't the ones who made the mess, but as my friend Old Blue told me, 'each generation of children will need to be taught how to properly care for the environment'."

Everyone in the class jumped up clapping. Mrs. Carlson gave Andie a hug.

Jeffrey Johnson raised his hand. Andie held her breath, worried about what wisecrack he was going to make. He surprised her by asking, "What can we do? We need to do something!"

Andie's classmates all began to talk at once.

Mrs. Carlson knew she could not ignore their enthusiasm. Ideas flooded her mind: art projects, poetry, science experiments, letter writing. But only one week remained to the school year, and it was already filled with games and paperwork.

Her mind quickly settled on one possibility, and she put the idea to a vote: "Shall we spend field day this Thursday working to save the Saint Jones, or shall we devote it to beating the 4th graders in kickball?"

The vote was unanimous.

That evening, Mrs. Carlson stayed at school late to organize a walking field trip to Legislative Hall. Meanwhile, every household in town who had a child in Mrs. Carlson's class got a lesson from their 5th grader about Silver Lake and the Saint Jones River.

Diving Deeper

Water tends to flow south in Delaware, and groundwater flows into rivers, ditches, the bay, and the ocean.

The area of land and water where water flows over or under, is called a "watershed." Delaware has four large watersheds: The Piedmont Basin watershed in northern Delaware, the Chesapeake Bay watershed in western Delaware, the Delaware Bay watershed in eastern Delaware, and the Inland Bays/Atlantic Ocean watershed in southern Delaware. These four large watersheds are broken down into 45 smaller watersheds. The St. Jones Watershed is located in central Delaware and drains into the Delaware Bay.

Whatever we do on the surface of the ground generally sinks down and goes into our groundwater. Anything that gets absorbed into the ground, gets absorbed into the water and eventually ends up in our drinking water.

Native plants tend to have longer roots than non-native plants and their long roots can absorb and filter out pollutants.

Wetlands filter pollution and absorb chemicals. In addition, wetlands act like a sponge when it rains and keep other areas from flooding.

Over time, Delaware has lost almost half of its wetlands and forests. Both can be restored. One of the largest wetland restoration projects in the U.S. is occurring in Delaware at the Prime Hook National Wildlife Refuge where scientists are studying the impact of new plantings, and other efforts which they hope will become a model for restoring wetlands throughout the world. (Morrison).

CHAPTER 24

The General Assembly

Legislative Hall was bustling with lobbyists and legislators debating various bills when Mrs. Carlson's fifth grade class entered the building. Mrs. Carlson had been able to secure a meeting with the governor, and the governor had arranged a special session with the legislators.

Each child had dressed up – even Andie. Her purple dress matched the purple headband that kept her curls out of her face. She was so excited that she barely noticed how much her shiny black shoes pinched her toes.

The governor welcomed the large group into her spacious office and asked what she could do for them. Mrs. Carlson introduced Andie. Andie took a deep breath and gave a shortened version of the presentation she had given to her classmates. Each child then held up a home-made poster and read a fact about water.

The governor praised the children for their efforts

and vowed to do everything in her power to help clean up the lake and the river and asked them to do the same.

The children repeated their presentation first for the Senate and then for the House of Representatives. Both chambers gave the children standing ovations. One state senator told the children about some laws the legislature had already passed to help protect the environment. He explained that sometimes it was hard to get people to change their behaviors, even when it was the law. He said, "If everyone could hear this presentation, they would understand the need for change."

The governor's staff had arranged a pizza party for the children in the legislative cafeteria. Lawmakers gathered around the children congratulating them and asking them questions. A few had never heard of "algae blooms," and a few more had not realized what caused them.

A newspaper reporter moved over to listen. He asked Mrs. Carlson a few questions and she turned him over to Andie.

The happy, chatty group returned to school,

136

walking on the wide sidewalks along the Saint Jones River.

Andie and Lily walked barefoot, side by side, carefully avoiding goose poop along the way. Mrs. Carlson caught up to them and said, "Andie Grove, you are a powerful speaker with a powerful dream. I know you are going to make this dream of yours come true."

Andie beamed, hugging her crumpled posters to her chest. Out of the corner of her eye, she saw a flash of blue. There he was, standing still, camouflaged beside a dead tree limb, looking right at Andie. She smiled at him, and he nodded.

Diving Deeper

Delaware students have led efforts to ban plastic drinking straws and plastic bags. They were responsible for getting the Delaware General Assembly to name the ladybug as the State's insect, the tiger swallowtail as the State's butterfly, the belemnite as the State's official fossil, and the grey fox as the State's wildlife animal.

All states except Nebraska have bicameral state legislatures that consist of a Senate and a House of Representatives. Nebraska is unicameral with just a Senate. Twenty-five states use the name "State Legislature." Nineteen states use the name "General Assembly" or "Legislative Assembly." Massachusetts and New Hampshire use the term "The General Court." Regardless of the title, these are the places where laws and state budgets are passed.

CHAPTER 25

Dreams

That night, Andie went to bed happy and exhausted. She quickly fell into a deep sleep and dreamed she was playing Marco Polo with Lily in Silver Lake. The water was so clear she could see her feet. Small children splashed along the edge of the lake as a lifeguard watched carefully from the freshly painted stand. Colorful towels blanketed the beach. Shiny kayaks glided gracefully along the Saint Jones River. The air was filled with the smell of hamburgers sizzling on the grill.

A great blue heron soared overhead. Andie looked up as a feather floated down toward her. A distant voice called to her.

"Andie! Wake up!"

What was Harry doing in her dream?

Andie looked at her picture on the front page of the newspaper that Harry had thrown onto her bed. Then she stretched and smiled. Summer was here. She had discovered her voice and her dream, and she had passed the 5th grade.

She looked toward the window to see what sort of a day it was. Sunlight glinted through the trees, a warm breeze blew, and a blue feather lay on the windowsill next to her bed.

Diving Deeper

Recent progress:

Water quality is continuously monitored at Silver Lake in three locations: At Fork Branch (the source of the Saint Jones River), Silver Lake beach, and the spillway at the dam. The water is monitored for temperature, pH, salinity, fecal bacteria, dissolved oxygen, total nitrogen, and phosphorus.

The data collected at Silver Lake show that total nitrogen and phosphorus have declined over the past two decades which suggests that farms, golf courses, residents, and the city are being more careful with their fertilizers.

In 2014, tests showed that the levels of PCBs in fish tissue in the Saint Jones River had fallen over time. The limit for how many 8 ounce servings of fish a person was allowed to consume, was raised from two to four.

Most of Delaware's power plants have stopped burning coal for electricity. When coal is burned, mercury is released into the air, and falls to the ground and into the water. Mercury is highly toxic to humans.

143

Coir logs have been placed along sections of the Saint Jones River to help establish wetland edges. A coir log is a roll of coconut fiber wrapped in jute mesh that is placed along the river bank. Over time, the "log" biodegrades as newly planted vegetation takes root.

Further national, state, and local actions that are needed:

Educate people about how their actions can impact the watershed.

Reclaim/rebuild more wetlands.

Address continuing problems with runoff of sediment and stormwater.

Monitor new development projects to ensure that runoff is carefully and effectively controlled.

Clean up waste sites, and avoid the creation of future waste sites.

Improve sewage treatment and pumping systems.

Apply best practices on farms to balance what the soil needs with what crops need in order to improve water quality.

Continue to support and enforce environmental laws.

Water-Related Vocabulary

Aquifer - porous rock below earth's surface which contains a large amount of groundwater.

Bog - a wetland with poor soil and high peat content.

Brackish - somewhat salty water.

Estuary - where the river meets the sea. Shellfish live here in the mixture of fresh water and salty seawater.

Flood Plain - low-lying ground, formed of mainly river sediments, that lies along a river and is subject to flooding.

Groundwater - water that lies below the surface of the land.

Invasive plant - a plant, usually non-native, that spreads rapidly, and crowds out other plants.

Marsh - a nutrient-rich wetland that supports a variety of reeds and grasses.

Native plant - a plant that has developed naturally over hundreds or thousands of years in an area.

Non-Native plant - a plant that has been introduced, either on purpose or by accident, to a new area.

Nonpoint source pollution - pollution that is picked up and carried by rain or melting snow and deposited into rivers or ground water. It does not come from one specific source such as an industrial or sewage plant.

Nitrogen and phosphorus - chemicals commonly found in fertilizers, manure, and sewage. They are important for plants, but when there is too much of either in a river, they cause algae blooms which keep the sun from reaching the plants on the bottom of the river. When the algae begins to decay, bacteria absorbs the oxygen that is in the water and releases ammonia which kills fish and other animals that live in the water (*Delaware Livable Lawns*).

Point Source Pollution - pollution that comes from an identifiable point such as a sewage plant or a factory.

Runoff - rainwater that runs over the ground, picking up particles that end up in bodies of water.

Sediment - matter which settles to the bottom of a river.

Stormwater - water from rainstorms which runs off roofs, streets, sidewalks, driveways, and other hard surfaces.

Sustainable - able to last a long time without harming the environment.

Swamp - a wetland that supports woody plants and trees.

Tributary - a small river which joins a larger river.

Watershed - area that drains into a river or another body of water.

Wetland - saturated land consisting of marshes or swamps, sometimes called a bog, bayou, or delta.

How You Can Help Protect and Conserve Water

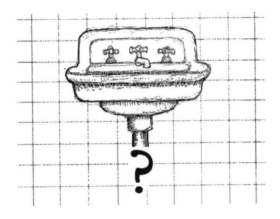

Find out where your water comes from.

Turn off the faucet while you brush your teeth.

Take showers rather than baths.

Take shorter showers.

Do not flush kitty litter down the toilet.

If you have a dog, always pick up its poop. Seal the waste in a bag and throw it into a garbage can. Dog poop has bacteria which can be absorbed through your lawn into the ground water. According to *Delaware Livable Lawns*, "The Environmental Protection Agency estimates that a population of 100 dogs would contribute enough bacteria in two to three days to temporarily close a bay and the surrounding area within 20 miles to swimming and shell fishing."

Do not flush anything other than human waste down the toilet.

Create less garbage by recycling paper, glass, metal, and plastics and by composting food scraps.

Remember to Reduce, Recycle, and Re-use.

Buy products with less packaging.

Use a re-usable water bottle.

Trees help clean pollutants from the soil and keep soil from eroding. Volunteer to help at a community tree planting event.

Volunteer to help with community waterways clean ups.

Share what you know and what you learn with your friends.

Write letters/emails to your legislators.

Ask adults to:

Choose laundry detergents and cleaners that contain low or no-phosphorus.

Install water-saving devices, such as low-flow shower heads.

Run the dishwasher and washing machine with full loads only.

Dispose of used oil, antifreeze, medicines, paints, and other household chemicals properly. If these are flushed or poured down the drain, they will end up in the watershed and in our drinking water. Contact Delaware Solid Waste Authority (DSWA) at 1-800-404-7080, or view their website (https://dswa.com) for more information about disposing of waste.

Consume less meat and dairy because a lot of water is used in their production.

If you have a septic system, have it checked for leaks.

Keep the storm drains near your house clear of garbage or debris.

Plant a rain garden that can catch and filter stormwater through the soil.

Install a rain barrel to catch water from the roof to use on your garden.

Plant your garden with native plants that do not need to be watered (except when they are first planted).

Mow the lawn at a height of 3 inches or higher and leave the clippings on the lawn to break down and fertilize the plants.

Fertilize the lawn responsibly. Do it in the fall and not when rain is in the forecast. Have your soil tested to find out if your lawn needs it. Soil testing kits and information are available at the Delaware Cooperative Extension (extension.udel.edu).

Replace your lawn with native perennials. Native trees

and plants have deep roots which can help hold sediment in place and slow down the absorption of storm water into the ground. (Plus, pollinators and insects that are good for the entire ecosystem prefer native plants to anything that is not native to the area.)

Blue's River Bibliography

Banyard, Antonia and Paula Ayer. *Water Wow! An Infographic Exploration.* 2016. Annick Press.

Blagg, G. Daniel. *Dover: A Pictorial History.* 1980. Donning Company Publishers, Virginia Beach.

Bupp, Susan L. *Hickory Bluff and the Saint Jones River Landscape.* April, 2000. Cultural Resources Department, Parsons. Fairfax, VA. Paper presented at the Society for American Archaeology Meetings, Philadelphia.

Butler, Robert W. *The Great Blue Heron.* 1997. University of British Columbia Press.

Clark, Allen B. *This is Good Country: A History of the Amish of Delaware, 1915-1988.* 1988. Gordonville Print Shop. Gordonville, PA.

Czerwinski, Eric. *Housing the Influx of Military Families Assigned to Dover Air Force Base in the Dover and Camden Communities of Kent Country, Delaware, 1952-1955: A Historic Context.* 2014. Delaware State University Historical Preservation Graduate Program.

Delaware Livable Lawns. Delawarelivablelawns.org.

Doerrfeld, Dean with David L. Ames, Bernard L. Herman, Rebecca J. Siders. *The Delaware Ship and Boat Building Industry, 1830-1940: An Historic Context.* 1994. University of Delaware.

Dunham, Margaret Raubacher. *Woodburn, Kings Court, Hall House: The Houses and the People that Made Them Homes - A 200 Year History.* July, 2001. Friends of The Delaware Public Archives.

Edwards, Pamela C. and Rebecca Siders. *The Changing Landscape of the St. Jones Neck Under the Influence of the Dickinson Family, 1680-1850: An Exhibit Script.* August, 1994. Center for Historic Architecture and Engineering. College of Urban Affairs and Public Policy, University of Delaware, Newark, DE.

Facts and Figures about Materials, Waste and Recycling: Plastics: Material-Specific Data. May 7, 2019. United States Environmental Protection Agency. *epa.gov.*

George, Pam. *Shipwrecks of the Delaware Coast: Tales of Pirates, Squalls, and Treasure.* 2010. The History Press. Charleston, NC.

Hancock, Harold B. *A History of Kent County, Delaware.* 1976. Dover Litho Printing Co. Dover, DE.

Hancock, James. *Herons of North America: Their World in Focus.* 2000. Academic Press. San Diego, CA.

Hanmer, Trudy J. *Water Resources.* 1985. Franklin Watts. New York, NY.

Heite, Edward F. and Cara L. Blume, *Archaeological and Historical Discoveries in Connection With Scarborough Road, Dover, Kent County, Delaware.* Delaware Department of Transportation Project 83-012001. FHWA Federal Aid Project M 1036 (1); Delaware Department of Transportation Archaeology Series Number 91. Heite Consulting, Camden, Delaware. 1992.

Historical Resources of St. Jones Neck, November, 1978. National Register of Historic Places Inventory - Nomination Form, United States Department of the Interior, National Park Service, Item #8, Pages 9 - 17.

History of the St. Jones River. DNREC. Delaware National Estuarine Research Reserve. Power Point.

Holland, Randy J. *Delaware's Destiny Determined by Lewes.* 2013. Delaware Heritage Press.

Jackson, James B. *The Early Settlement and Founding of Kent County Delaware 1671-1683.* 1983. Kent County Delaware Tricentennial Commission. Dover, DE

Jackson, James B. *The Golden Fleece Tavern: The Birthplace of the First State.* 1987. The Friends of Old Dover, Inc.

Logan, Algernon Sydney. *Amy Warren. A Tale of the Bay Shore.* 1934. Philadelphia National Publishing Company. Philadelphia, PA.

Min, Shirley. *Health of Delaware's Waterways.*

May, 2016. WHYY. YouTube.

Morrison, Jim. *Coastal Recovery: Bringing a Damaged Wetland Back to Life.* May 9, 2019. YaleEnvironment360. https://e360.yale.edu.

Newton, James E. *Black Americans in Delaware: An Overview.* <u>A History of African Americans of Delaware and Maryland's Eastern Shore.</u> Edited by Carole Marks. 1999. Delaware Heritage Press.

Norwood, John R. *We Are Still Here! The Tribal Saga of New Jersey's Nanticoke and Lenape Indians.* 2007. Native New Jersey Publications.

Oates, Michael. *The Price of Progress...The Promise of Protection: The Saint Jones River.* 2012. Video. Delaware National Estuarine Research Reserve.

Passmore, Joanne O., Charles Maske, and Daniel Harris. *Three Centuries of Delaware Agriculture.* 1978. The Delaware State Grange and the Delaware American Revolution Bicentennial Commission.

Sammak, Dr. Emil G. and Don O. Winslow, eds. *Dover, The First Two Hundred and Fifty Years, 1717-1967: A Brief History of Dover, Delaware, Illustrated.* 1967. City of Dover. Delaware.

Six Tricentennial Views of Kent County, Delaware, Number Six: A Tricentennial View of Dover 1683 - 1983. 1985. Delaware Humanities Forum and Dover Public Library. Delaware.

Slavin, Peter F. and Timothy A. Slavin. *Images*

of America: Dover. 2003. Arcadia Publishing. Dover, NH.

Van Sant, Douglas Andrew. *Hometown: Reminiscences of a 1940s Dover, Delaware Childhood.* 2005. Dover Litho Printing.

Weslager, C.A. *Delaware's Forgotten Folk: The Story of the Moors and Nanticokes.* 1943. University of Pennsylvania Press. Philadelphia, PA.

Wiggins, Brig. Gen. Kennard R. Jr. *Dover AFB History.* Research paper, courtesy of Mr. Harry Heist, 2018.

Williams, William H. *Man and Nature in Delaware: An Environmental History of the First State 1631-2000.* 2008. Delaware Heritage Press. Dover, DE.

Acknowledgments

Blue's River has been a labor of love and learning which would not have been possible without the help of many people.

First and foremost, this book would not exist without Jim McGiffin's love, encouragement, proofreading, and day job. I love you, Jim!

Marsha Holler, your beautiful illustrations brought this book to life.

Jan Crumpley, your inspiration, encouragement, and friendship helped make this book a reality.

Theo "Three Winds" Braunskill, former Councilwoman and Member of the Lenape Elder's Council, thank you for fact-checking the chapter on the Lenape.

Margaret Raubacher Dunham, your passion for and extensive knowledge of Dover's history, your help with research at the Delaware Public Archives, and your feedback on early drafts make you one of my heroes.

Lynn Edler, YA guru, thank you for your friendship, edits, and encouragement.

Heidi Greene, and the Campus Community School staff, thank you for allowing us to use your classrooms as the model for Andie's classroom.

Gary Knox, thank you for your enthusiastic support and creative suggestions.

Sarah Monsma, your editing assistance was invaluable.

Laura Parks, thank you for your extensive comments, feedback, grammar rules, and grammar lessons!

Chazz Salkin (retired director of the Delaware Division of Parks and Recreation and current board member of the Kent County Conservancy), thank you for your multi-layered assistance on this project which included a heronry field trip, numerous connections to folks at the Department of Natural Resources and Environmental Control (DNREC), and editing one of the first drafts of this book.

Thank you Susan Salkin, retired Deputy Director of the Delaware Division of the Arts; Roxanne Stanulis, Program Officer for Artist Programs and Services at the Delaware Division of the Arts; and Paul Weagraff, Director of the Delaware Division of the Arts, for your guidance and support throughout this project.

Douglas A. Van Sant, thank you for fact-checking the earliest draft.

Thank you Josh Barth, Carolyn Courtney, and Scott Cole — all employees of the City of Dover — for responding to dozens of questions.

Thank you to the many people currently working for or retired from DNREC, who taught me about great blue herons, the Saint Jones River, and the Saint Jones Watershed: Chris Bennett, John Cargill, Bruce Cole, Kimberly Cole, Audrey DeRose-Wilson, Rick Greene, Katie Huegel, Lyle Jones and Stephen Williams.

Gratitude goes out to Alice Guerrant from the Division of Historical and Cultural Affairs for sharing National Register information about historic properties in the watershed; Ruth Ann Purchase for helping with Lenape linguistics; Kelly Valencik, Coastal Training Program Coordinator for the Delaware National Estuarine Research Reserve, for sharing some Saint Jones River history; Larry Koewing, Air Mobility Command Museum (AMCM) Photographer and Photo Archivist at the Dover Air Force Base (DAFB), for sharing aerial photographs and for connecting me to Harry Heist, Archivist for the AMCM who shared Ken Wiggins' thorough history of DAFB and Eric Czerwinski's excellent paper on DAFB Housing; and Gloria Henry, Site Supervisor for the John Dickinson Plantation for information about slavery and the plantation.

Thanks and apologies to all the helpful folks at the St. Jones Reserve whose names I never learned, and to anyone else I may have inadvertently left out.

And finally, Lois Hoffman, I am eternally grateful for your patience and skill in shepherding *Blue's River* through its final stages of production.

This book is supported, in part, by a grant from the Delaware Division of the Arts, a state agency, in partnership with the National Endowment for the Arts. The Division promotes Delaware arts events on DelawareScene.com.

Made in the USA
Middletown, DE
13 October 2021